Archway Publishing books may be ordered through booksellers or by contacting:

Archway Publishing
1663 Liberty Drive
Bloomington, IN 47403
www.archwaypublishing.com
844-669-3957

Because of the dynamic nature of the Internet, any web addresses or links contained in this book may have changed since publication and may no longer be valid. The views expressed in this work are solely those of the author and do not necessarily reflect the views of the publisher, and the publisher hereby disclaims any responsibility for them.

Interior Image Credit: Darlene Daniels

Scripture quotations marked NIV are taken from the Holy Bible, New International Version®, NIV®. Copyright © 1973, 1978, 1984 by Biblica, Inc.™ Used by permission of Zondervan. All rights reserved worldwide.

Scripture quotations marked MSG or The Message are taken from The Message. Copyright 1993, 1994, 1995, 1996, 2000, 2001, 2002. Used by permission of NavPress Publishing Group.

ISBN: 978-1-6657-4121-7 (sc)
ISBN: 978-1-6657-4120-0 (hc)
ISBN: 978-1-6657-4122-4 (e)

Library of Congress Control Number: 2023905404

Print information available on the last page.

Archway Publishing rev. date: 06/20/2023

Glorious Glimpses of Heaven

Illustrated in watercolor

by Darlene Daniels

This book is the result of a trauma in my life – the sudden death of my dear husband of 46 years. For four months before his death God gave me a thirst for learning about heaven. That search led to reading about near death experiences. After he died, all my newfound knowledge about heaven was a tremendous comfort to me. I knew my Mugsy was forever at peace in the arms of Jesus. But more than that, I had visions in my mind of what he might be experiencing in heaven.

God led me to create this book, over the course of a year, to be a comfort to others and a "picture of heaven". God even led me to learn to watercolor to show impressions of heaven. So the illustrations are a newly learned skill in my life. One that I love. I dedicate this book to Mugsy and to all of our lost loves. May we have peace in the assurance of where they are and that we will someday soon see them again. This time forever.

Glorious Glimpses of Heaven is a look into heaven through the eyes of people who have had near death experiences. God has given these people a rare look into the future that awaits them in heaven. Along with their quotes are Scriptures that correlate to what they have experienced.

A look into the pages of this book will inspire and delight you, as well as bring you comfort if you have lost a loved one, or want to know what is waiting for you when your time on this earth is over.

ANGELS

For He will command his angels
concerning you
to guard you in all your ways.

Psalm 91:11 NIV

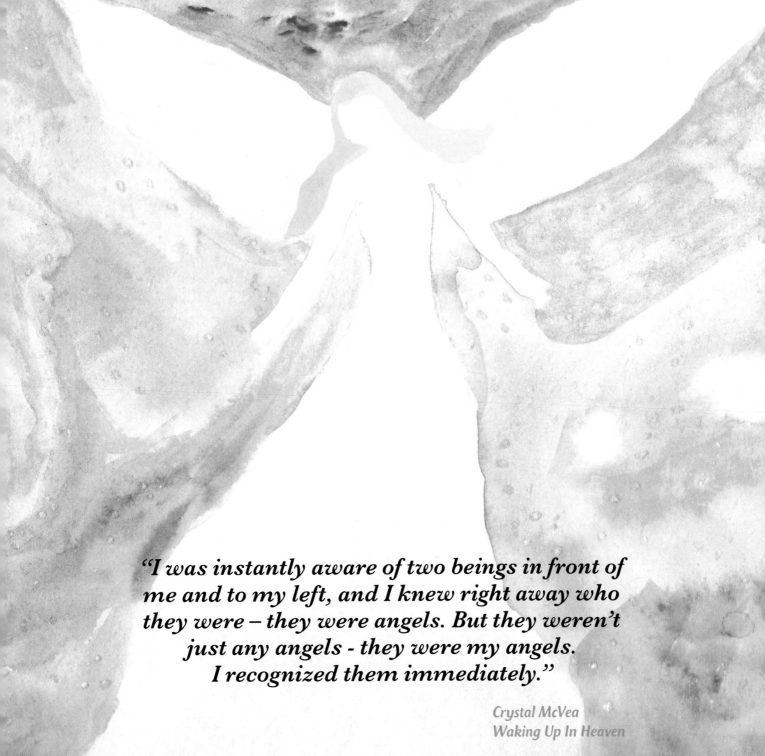

"I was instantly aware of two beings in front of me and to my left, and I knew right away who they were – they were angels. But they weren't just any angels - they were my angels. I recognized them immediately."

Crystal McVea
Waking Up In Heaven

4

FUTURE IN HEAVEN

Because Jesus was raised from the dead, we've been given brand new life and have everything to live for, including a future in heaven.

1Peter 1:3,4 MSG

"*A strong sense of belonging filled my heart; I never wanted to leave. Somehow I knew I was made for this place, and this place was made for me.*"

Dale Black
Flight To Heaven:
A Plane Crash

6

FACE TO FACE

Now we see but a poor reflection as in a mirror; then we shall see face to face. Now I know in part, then I shall know fully, even as I am fully known.

1Corinthians 13:12 NIV

"What I experienced in heaven was so real and so lucid and so utterly intense, it made my experiences on earth seem hazy and out of focus."

Crystal McVea
Waking Up In Heaven

HIS PRESENCE

His body was like chrysolite, His face like
lightning, His eyes like flaming torches,
His arms and legs like the gleam of
burnished bronze, and His voice like the
sound of a multitude.

Daniel 10:5,6 NIV

"I was so consumed by His presence that I dropped to my knees and looked up at Him. He is so glorious, so beautiful. All light inside of light."

Khalida
From Imagine Heaven
John Burke

10

HIS LOVE

What no eye has seen, what no ear
has heard, and what no human mind
has conceived – the things God has
prepared for those who love Him.

1Corinthians 2:9 NIV

"It was a feeling of absolute purity and perfection, of something completely unblemished and unbroken, and being immersed in it filled me with the kind of peace and assurance I'd never known on earth. It was like being bathed in love."

Crystal McVea
Waking Up In Heaven

INTIMACY

Before I formed you in the womb I knew you,
before you were born, I set you apart."

Jeremiah 1:5 NIV

"He looks straight through you and into you…He knew all there was to know about you."

Lisa
From Imagine Heaven
John Burke

"…all the junk that cluttered my identity on Earth instantly fell away, revealing for the first time ever, the real me."

Crystal McVea
Waking Up In Heaven

14

HOME

How lovely is your dwelling place,
O Lord Almighty!

Psalm 84:1 NIV

"It was a brightness I didn't just see, but felt. And it felt familiar, like something I remembered, or even recognized. The best way to put it is this: I was home."

Eben Alexander
Proof of Heaven

16

LIGHT

The city does not need the sun or the moon
to shine on it, for the Glory of God gives it
light, and the Lamb is its lamp.

Revelation 21:23 NIV

"Somehow I knew that light and life
and love were connected and interrelated…
Remarkably, the light didn't shine on things,
but through them. Through the grass.
Through the trees. Through the wall.
And through the people."

Dale Black
Flight To Heaven:
A Plane Crash

18

RESTORED

He will wipe every tear from their eyes.
There will be no more death or mourning or
crying or pain, for the old order of things
has passed way.

Revelation 21:4 NIV

"God keeps records because all our loss and suffering will one day be restored in Heaven."

Crystal McVea
Waking Up In Heaven

NEW BODY

But our citizenship is in heaven. And we eagerly
await a Savior from there, the Lord Jesus Christ,
who…will transform our lowly bodies so that
they will be like His glorious body.

Philippians 3:20,21 NIV

"Not only will we be free of the pains and worries of this earthly body, we will feel young again! Remember what it was like to have endless energy as a child? Recall the strength and stamina of those teen years? Imagine a new body that feels even better than that!"

John Burke
Imagine Heaven

CREATION

…the creation itself will be liberated
from its bondage to decay…

Romans 8:20 NIV

"The plants there move and sing when I move and talk. It seems as if they can think. Animals are not like here. They listen to me and they're not afraid of me, so I can pet them whenever I want...I also fly on top of huge birds..."

Akiane Kramarik
Akiane: Her life,
Her Art, Her Poetry

24

MUSIC

Then I looked and heard the voice of many
angels, numbering thousands upon thousands,
and ten thousand times ten thousand…
In a loud voice they sang:

"Worthy is the Lamb, who was slain, to receive
power and wealth and wisdom and strength
and honor and glory and praise!"

Revelation 5:11,12 NIV

"Somehow the music in heaven calibrated everything...Music was everywhere...the joy of music could be felt...I had the feeling I was made for music."

Dale Black
Flight To Heaven:
A Plane Crash

WORSHIP

Come let us bow down in worship, let us
kneel before the Lord our Maker; for He is
our God and we are the people of His
pasture, the flock under His care.

Psalm 95:6,7 NIV

"You will completely surrender to His greatness. You will have an overwhelming desire to praise and worship Him with all your might. Joyously, happily, you will praise God with every fiber of your existence."

Crystal McVea
Waking Up In Heaven

MY FATHER'S HOUSE

In my Father's house are many
rooms…I am going to prepare a
place for you…and will come back
and take you to be with me…"

John 14:1-7 NIV

"Between the central part of the city and the city walls were groupings of brightly colored, picture perfect homes in small quaint towns... Each home was customized and unique from the others, yet blended harmoniously..."

Dale Black
Flight To Heaven:
A Plane Crash

30

GOD'S RAINBOW

He looked like fire; and brilliant light
surrounded Him. Like the appearance
of a rainbow in the clouds on a rainy day,
so was the radiance around Him.

Ezekiel 1:27,28 NIV

"It was an awesome, colorful light show. Colors flashed, like sheets of lightning... Awesome rainbows of inexpressible colors flowed over, around and into the city-cube."

Ed Gaulden
Heaven:
A Joyful Place

RIVER OF LIFE

The Spirit and the bride say, "Come!"…
Whoever is thirsty come; and
whoever wishes, let him take
the free gift of the Water of Life.

Revelation 22:17 NIV

"As we walked into the River of Life,
it got deeper and deeper until finally
the surface of the river was over the
top of our heads. We were still breathing
and so then I got the understanding this
is the flowing of the Spirit of God;
it is a manifestation of the Spirit of God."

Dr. Gary L. Wood
A Place Called Heaven

34

God gives us glimpses of heaven here on earth. The rainbow is what is over God's throne in heaven; the crystal clear waters and rivers are glimpses of the River of Life. The animals that we love as family are examples of the animals that all abide together in peace; and they represent unconditional love. The jewelry we wear here on earth is a small example of the jewels around God's throne. The brilliance of the sun is a foreshadow of the light of God a thousand times brighter, only we will be able to look at it without hurting our eyes. The beauty of plants, as beautiful as they are, won't compare to the "living" plants in heaven, with colors beyond those we currently see, vibrant and alive from within. Gold is treasured on earth, but God's throne is a gold that is clear and pure.

Then there's music that moves our spirit and touches our soul. This is perhaps the most important gift on earth that foreshadows the worshipping of God in heaven, where the music will become part of us. Church is probably the closest we come on earth to what it will be like to worship God in unison; to feel connected to each other, but at the same time connected to God.

Family gives us a great sense of belonging, but when we get to heaven we will finally be home. We will know that we belong to the family of God.

Printed in the United States
by Baker & Taylor Publisher Services